HOW TO TURN YOUR PASSIONS, SKILL SET AND TALENTS INTO PROFITS.

RICHARD.A.KING

All rights reserved. No part of this publication may be reproduced, distributed or transmitted in any form or by any means, including photocopying, recording, or other electronic or mechanical method, without the prior written permission of the publisher, except in the case of brief quotations embodied in critic reviews and certain other non-commercial uses permitted by copyright law.

Copyright Richard.A. King, 2023

Table of Contents

.Introduction
.Chapter 1
.Chapter 2
.Chapter 3
.Chapter 4
.Chapter 5
.Chapter 6
.Chapter 7
.Chapter 8

Introduction

You must fulfill a need for others in order to convert your passion into profit. Sadly, people and organizations do not particularly care if you are able to follow your passions. They spend their money on things that gratify their desires, including people, services, and objects. However, you might be able to gather a group of competent clients who share your interests and are in desperate need of your knowledge and abilities. In addition to being very eager to pay handsomely for it, people will also follow. Finding a strategy to attract them is the only issue.

In business, what does passion imply?

An entrepreneur's passion is a powerful force that pushes them to transform an idea or path into a successful business. For an enterprise to succeed, money and passion must coexist.

Why do you intend to turn your passions into a business?

Any necessary compromises can be made more tolerable by developing a career around something you enjoy and having a strong sense of purpose. It can also help keep you motivated when things are tough and make your wins even sweeter because you may be taking steps to stoke your passion and complete your purpose.

What are the benefits of basing your business on your interests?

The most effective marketers that convert passion into profit focus on their strengths and seek out individuals who share their ideals and interests in order to fill in the gaps. This is not only a successful business strategy, but research also shows that people who exploit their abilities at work are happier and healthier.

We may move on to the first path, which includes specific procedures and reliable facts on how precisely we want to develop and maintain a successful firm, now that we comprehend the meaning, causes, roles, and significance that our passions perform in creating a successful enterprise. They are as follows:

—-Creating a circle:

One of the most crucial components of your growth and personal development in the direction of your goals is your circle of influence. Your circle of influence matters whether you're a small-business owner, an entrepreneur, a tech expert, a wealthy person, or are genuinely working to grow your various businesses or legacy.
Although the phrase "circle of affect" has been used to describe a variety of unusual concepts, I use the phrase

"circle of impact" to refer to the group of people who are impacting you. Your circle of influence is made up of the people you spend time with—those whose strength, insights, endeavors, thoughts, and thoughts have an effect on how you perceive and behave.

All individuals have a circle of influence, even if they haven't worked hard to consciously create it. By default, I take it for granted that the people in your regular circle will affect how they interact with one another. The number of people in the organization may vary, but it may include your employees, mentors, mentees, or even your customers and members of your own family. Though not everyone in your circle of influence will affect you equally when it does, there is no denying that you are still affected by them. For instance, you might spend a lot of time with your partner or young child. It is correct that they won't be "influencing you professionally" if they are no longer interested in your business or a portion of your professional operation. However, you will be impacted by and affected by their electrical levels, attitudes, behaviors, and perception structures.

Therefore, it's imperative to include everyone. Think about the top five to ten people you interact with the most. These are the people in your immediate social circle. There are few steps you must do to get started if you decide you want to build your circle:

1. Consciously choose humans:

A conscious system that requires you to actively seek them out is the process of choosing which people to include in your sphere of influence. By visiting events where you know those people may be present, striking up discussions, networking on social media, and cultivating current relationships that fit those categories, you can achieve your goals. There are three categories of people I advise picking for your circle of influence:

1. Consciously choose humans:

(a) Individuals with more experience than you:

There is great value in surrounding oneself with a few people who have more experience than you have in your selected profession; this is the first thing most people think of when they hear the phrase "circle of affect." This is probably a single mentor or a group of people you may talk to for advice, inspiration, and insight.

Mentorship (b)

Legacy-building is greatly aided by mentoring. It can, in my opinion, also promote mutual growth in addition to giving back to your community and profession. Additionally, mentees have the potential to become future colleagues.

(c) Individuals that have no connection to your industry:

Not every person in your circle of influence needs to work in your field or be in the same trade. In fact, I think it's crucial that you surround yourself with at least a few non-believers. Knowing others in a same job can have advantages, but there can also be disadvantages. It can encourage rivalry, constrained thinking, burnout, and it can cause you to become enmeshed in an idea bubble or echo chamber.

As a result, it's crucial to involve people from entirely unrelated professions in your circle of influence. These people can give you perspective, serve as a reminder of the wider picture, and provide your brain with a break from the constant repetition of thoughts linked to your professional activities.

2. Establish connections with those in your sphere of influence:

The exciting part can begin once you've determined who you want in your sphere of influence: cultivating relationships with them.

Spend some time with these people. Make a frequent email correspondence, brainstorm, meet over video chats or the phone, and go out for dinner or drinks. Gain insight from them and take in their vitality. You'll gain more from these relationships if you put more effort into them.

3. Form a community by gathering your circle:

A powerful approach to build something greater than oneself is through community. Bring together as many of the people in your circle of influence as you can. This can happen during a dinner or just at a casual or skilled mixer.

It changes everything when you bring your circle together. You establish a group mind-share that is the ideal setting for coming up with fresh concepts, surmounting challenges, and exchanging brilliant ideas. The more frequently you can gather your circle, even if not everyone is present, the better. A mastermind effect can be created even at a typical meeting of just three people, allowing you to collaborate to develop, communicate, or simply grow as a group.

Chapter 2

How to lead your clients.

What does it mean to lead you on? Influence, motivation, and persuasion are key components of effective leadership. What has been accomplished is more important than which projects have been finished.

1. Recognize the values of your customers:

Always pay attention to what and how your consumers are communicating in order to learn what they value. Then, modify your strategy to meet their needs.

Some clients will need frequent one-on-one interactions with your company. Some people might not care too much about being seen; they just want to call you, place an order, and go about their day. While some will be searching for all the bells and whistles, some will be very price conscious. Try your best to continue hearing!

2. Show that you care:

People often want to interact on a personal level as well as a professional one. That is why being amiable and individual pays off. Discover what you have in common with consumers and talk about it; inquire about their children or wish them a happy birthday on the occasion; and follow up on important data.

Some people can remember information like that automatically, but if you can't, just record it in your contact list. Being genuine at all times is essential. Customers are able to discern when you aren't being sincere, according to Palin. "Consider employing someone if being a 'people person' isn't your strong suit."

3. Go at their speed:

Avoid wasting their time with small talk and polite conversation if they pick up the phone and are obviously pressed for time. However, if a consumer phones and requests to chat, be sure not to cut them off mid-sentence.

4. Use your brand as a compass:

Delivering on the promises your branding and marketing make regarding the client experience and your organization as a whole is crucial. If you pledge to be available to customers at all times, but when they call you, they can only reach your voicemail, you have broken your word.

The commitments you must make are intimately tied to the distinctive value proposition of your business. Consider a membership-based wholesaler as opposed to a high-end technology boutique. Both are providing exactly what their clients anticipate, despite the fact that the customer experience could not be more dissimilar between a large warehouse and individualized, attentive service.

5. Act in the manner you want to see:

The way you treat your employees sets the tone for how they should treat your clients. If you're constantly looking for ways to save expenses, your staff may also believe that they shouldn't be offering discounts or raising prices in other ways, which can go a long way toward exceeding client expectations.

6. Keep in mind that relationships develop over time.

Chapter. 3

—-How to capture your audience's interest.

The good news is that while it's no longer easy to capture a busy consumer's attention, it is now much harder than it was in the past. You merely wish to understand the process.

Here are a few expert pointers for accomplishing that and building the steadfast clientele you know you deserve.

1. Determine your goal's pain points:

When you engage in virtual advertising, it is possible for your target audience to come into your advertising content while they are already extremely busy, stressed out, or otherwise engaged.

And while it may be the true for an individual, they are much more focused on their immediate needs than they are on the rest of their environment.

It's crucial to catch your customers' attention by speaking to the issues that are currently on their minds.

What issues and concerns are your products intended to address?

Think about how you could frame your message to appeal to those who have those problems in mind.

2. Pay attention to your distinctive qualities:

The internet world is a noisy place, full of businesses that resemble one another everywhere.

Additionally, they are all offering the same outdated services or goods that your customers have been seeing for years. Your advertising campaigns must highlight the strategies you use if you're serious about capturing the attention of your potential customers.

Remember that your potential customers probably have had their issues, concerns, aspirations, and ambitions for a very long time.

They are likely receptive to discovering fresh or more effective approaches to dealing with those aspects of their lives.

So get to the meat of how your company differs from the competition, why your product is the solution your customer has been looking for, and what makes you a higher choice.

3. Make your objective meaningful:

Consider the last time you truly felt something after reading some online content or hearing a commercial.

It's possible that you briefly put an end to what you were doing because it caught your attention and you decided it was important or particularly relevant to you. Perhaps you too thought about it for a while after.

Your customers are of same character.

Emotions are more than just potent motivators. Additionally, it's crucial to make sure people remember your message long after they've consumed it and moved on with their life.

By appealing to your customer's emotions, you can also enhance the likelihood that they'll remember you when the time comes for them to make a purchase.

Motivate your audience by making them think, feel, or laugh. It's a great method to talk to them and develop enduring connections.

4. Embrace the excitement of video:

In terms of global-magnificence advertising, there is still a lot to be said for written internet content and beautiful images, but movies are red-hot right now and are only getting hotter as the day goes on.

Additionally, they often manage to hold people's attention while they scroll through their many timelines, which is a difficult task in today's society.

Once you've captured your audience's attention, make sure to hold onto it by keeping your movies succinct, sweet, and directly to the point.

Avoid using the old-school hard-sell method when creating video content for social media in favor of being entertaining or informative.

5. Make it easy to scan your textual content:

Although there will always be a need for smart, concise, well-written web content, it's critical to design yours with the modern consumer's short attention span in mind.

Avoid using lengthy justifications when a few simple words will suffice.

Whenever feasible, let charts, photographs, and other visuals speak for you. And to increase engagement, provide interactive content.

Always break up your content into manageable chunks so that readers may easily skim your work to find what they're looking for.

Every time it makes sense, use headers, subheadings, bold fonts, and bulleted lists.

Chapter. 4

---Gain their trust.

Once the third phase is complete, make every effort to earn their trust.
This means that gaining the trust of your consumers can help you not only retain them but also generate new leads and revenue through word-of-mouth. It is obvious that any firm should strive to increase client loyalty and trust. You may only do this if you interact with them fairly and are "totally honest."

Chapter 5

—- Create and maintain a community.

What is a community, exactly?

collaborating, networking, and providing support. Nothing beats bouncing ideas off another business owner, getting a second pair of eyes on a project, or just talking to someone who is going through a similar stage of life.

Not only that, but having a supportive, giving community will help your business develop considerably. Here are some ideas on how to develop and maintain one:

1. Bring your tribe together for a common cause:

When people are unified by a shared objective, cause, or conviction, they frequently feel as though they are a part of something greater than themselves. This might be as straightforward as everyone organizing the wedding of their dreams or as lofty as significantly altering their community's judicial system. Whatever it is, make it very apparent that your community is for a particular set of individuals who identify with a shared purpose they are pleased to support.

2. Invest time listening to community members on purpose:

Under the rule of a dictator, there is less of a sense of community and more of a democracy. Therefore, when members of your community ask for change, suggest a new procedure, or provide input... Attend to them! They won't feel appreciated if they don't feel heard... because for your tribe to flourish, each individual must feel like a valuable contributor.

3. Answer all remarks and direct messages:

This advice complements the previous one by demonstrating to your community that you value their opinions by reacting to comments and direct messages. As a result, every participant will be much more inclined to continue engaging, communicating, and being an active member of your community if they feel heard, appreciated, and replied to.

4. Make connections with the people in your community:

One of our favorite aspects of the Social Curator community is when members of it meet up with one another outside of our exclusive Facebook group, whether it be for a coffee date, mastermind, or Zoom hangout. These kinds of connections can be facilitated by the group's leader by suggesting that various members connect with one another, scheduling meet-ups so that they can interact in person, or setting up accountability partners for the group.

5. Provide assistance when required:

A giving, supportive leader (yes, YOU!) is the foundation of any giving, supportive group. Therefore, treat everyone in your community with kindness and empathy to create the kind of atmosphere you'd love to be a part of, whether it's giving advise to a member who has asked for it, alerting others when a member needs assistance, or making sure everyone feels inspired in their quest.

There you have it, 5 strategies to foster community in your company.

Chapter 6

—- Prepare the audience.

They are not psychologists, marketers. Most of them aren't, at least. However, some of the most successful advertising, marketing, and public relations initiatives in

history have utilized moral norms of decency. Manufacturers, business owners, and advertisers were able to have a better understanding of their target audience by frequently utilizing these notions, which has allowed the respective manufacturers to build stronger, more meaningful connections.
There are two kinds.

1. Classical conditioning

Psychology's concept of classical conditioning describes learning through repetition. Its ultimate goal is to induce a spontaneous response to a chosen situation by repeatedly exposing a subject (customer) to a chosen stimulus (an emblem, product, or service).

2. Operant conditioning

Operant conditioning, on the other hand, describes behavior changes brought on by studies that happen after a response. Most people are at least somewhat aware of this type of conditioning because it involves the use of reinforcement or punishment to control behavior. Numerous studies have demonstrated how effective this conditioning is on people as well. And in recent decades, behavioral conditioning has become a powerful tool for businesses and manufacturers looking to increase awareness and commitment.

—-CONDITIONING IN MARKETING

So how does all of this play out in marketing and advertising? In classical conditioning, the goal is to induce consumers to associate certain brands with a particular emotion or response. Operant conditioning most likely resembles a suggestion or a benefit, like "buy one, get one free."

For instance, a soda company has successfully associated their emblem with contentment and happiness. By connecting the beverage to activities that include physical activity and natural phenomena like sports, the sun, and the beach—things that make you thirsty. Customers all throughout the world have come to think of that logo as a thirst quencher. Therefore, there's a good chance you'll start thinking about their beverage if you're hot, if you've just exercised, or if you're on the beach.
Use any to promote your product in your neighborhood.

Chapter 7

—-Commit to monetizing.

Find the right tribe for your company, and you'll benefit from higher profitability, more lucrative possibilities, and a competitive edge. Additionally, the more you interact with your network, the more probable it is that they will continue to use your brand or perhaps return for more.

However, the main concern for most agencies is how to effectively monetize their online network. The next seven methods will put you on the right path.

1. Create a club website online:

One of the best ways to commercialize an internet network is through this strategy. You may capitalize on the interest your customers already have in your content by using membership websites.

You can start by creating freely available content for your website that draws in visitors and keeps them interested. When you see a need for your content to expand, you add a paywall to the mix. This will encourage your customers to sign up for paying memberships in order to access certain areas of exclusive content.

Through Tribe and Zapier, you can quickly add payment options for subscriptions to your website, giving your visitors the option to pay with Stripe or PayPal.

Finding the right pricing to charge for your premium subscribers is essential, and polling your network's members is one of the best ways to determine your content strategy.

2. Sell a web direction:

Running a web business is yet another outstanding way to monetize your network. In 2019, the online e-learning market was estimated to be pretty well worth about $1 billion. Its miles are anticipated to reach $167 billion in 2026.

Through courses, you may transform priceless expertise into a useful tool for your target audience. If your customers already like the advice you share on your network, they will be willing to take the risk of looking farther.

The right idea must be chosen if you want your online publications to be successful. Start by looking at your website analytics and determining which topics your visitors visit the most frequently.

Additionally, think about the types of issues that people working for your company encounter, and research what your rivals are doing to help clients who are similar to yours.

The closer you can get to your intended market, the better.

Remember that it's important to move past broad overviews of topics while building a web direction. Get deeply involved with a particular issue or circumstance that your customer is facing and give them a deal they can't get anywhere else.

3. Start an educational program :

Training packages are a terrific method to monetise your information, much like online manuals are. Self-improvement is a popular concept in the virtual world, and there are probably others in your network who have skills they'd like to develop with your help.

If you have expertise in a useful field, you may offer instruction without even having to develop a product first. Similar to consulting, training entails listening to the specific desires of your client and making recommendations that are relevant to them.

You can start with one-on-one encounters, in which people pay for a little period of time to help them with a specific issue.

If you find that many of your followers are dealing with the same issues, you may decide to launch a structured training program where people may sign up for huge webinar-style seminars. Giving group training is a great way to make extra money all at once, and you can even give one-on-one sessions concurrently.

4. Advertising:

This is another fantastic option for generating sales from a network. Native marketing and marketing are both included. Agencies of all sizes today need to strengthen their connections to their intended target market through marketing and marketing on various platforms.

This most well-known marketing method allows you to easily display a banner at the top of the domestic web page feed for your network.

Have sponsored content offered on your website as an additional option. For instance, if you manage a network dedicated to search engine marketing and an advertising company wants to sell their product there, they may make a blog post on your network outlining the top qualities to look for in a search engine marketing company.

This sponsored entry may link back to the website of the competing business and display its logo.

You may get a lot of manufacturers looking for promotional reach if your website or magazine already has a sizable following.

There are numerous ways to advertise it to your website and generate cash as a result. For instance, if you want to place a banner advertisement inside your network, you may ask the businesses that need to pay you to do so.

5. Request donations:

Consider donations if you don't want to promote your neighborhood and you can't think of any branded goods or specific items that you'd like to publicize.

Donations, as opposed to other forms of monetization that demand a like-for-like change in value, are all about fostering an enterprise's expansion. Your customers will be more likely to give to help your business flourish if you uphold principles that they share and respect.

You need a strong emotional connection with your target market that provides a few intangible qualities if you want to acquire donations.

If you can convince your audience that your information will help them increase the amount they sell on their own websites, for instance, you may be able to collect donations.

You may also persuade others to donate to your cause so you can continue making the movies they enjoy.

It's quite simple to implement donation opportunities in your community because all you need to do is use a shape builder to design a donation shape.

Don't forget to express gratitude to your target audience for the support they have given you in order to increase the likelihood that they will donate. A special way to show your appreciation is by placing a bonus sticky label that says "donor" on their member profile.

6. Start monetizing your community:

People will always be the most valuable asset a company can have. The more devoted supporters you amass for your brand or organization, the more effectively you may tap into their fervor and commitment for your business.

When your community is growing and successful, there are thousands of unique ways to make money off of it, whether you decide to sell books and coaching or brand products and sell them online.

The secret to your success may lie in thinking about how to make the most of your fans while maintaining the relationship you've established. In essence, you need to strike a balance between your drive to generate money and the popularity of your brand.

Chapter. 8

—- Create regular contents

We can all recognize successful people who seem to have everything in their virtual art lives fall into place without any problems. They never skip a beat and work tirelessly to find shareable content that attracts devoted fans. Most individuals are left wondering how they will be able to keep up with everything on the worldwide level.

The fact that those elders have perfected the technique of reducing their creative process makes it clear how they manage to turn their content into gold. They have set up a plan, established a schedule, and adhere to it consistently so that you can go through the movements while closing your eyes.

I want you to think about your content marketing approach in that way. No, I'm not saying you have to paint while your eyes are closed; rather, you should paint efficiently and sustainably.

The more streamlined your content creation process is, the easier it will be to maintain consistency in your output.

Examine the process now.

1. Compile a Running List of Your Thoughts:

Get into the habit of keeping all of these random (but valuable) thoughts in one special location that you can access at any time to make coming up with topics easier. Because you're much more likely to carry it with you wherever you go, I recommend using your smartphone or creating a list of all of your other devices that can sync with it (well, besides while the ones exquisite bathe thoughts strike).

Even if they seem minor, write down any ideas that come to mind. If you have the time to keep in mind the picture it can create for you, you may be able to take a simple idea and develop it later on.

Additionally, you'll quickly increase the range of options you have to choose from, which will be helpful when you visit and plan your schedule of events.

2. Make a calendar of content:

Being able to create shareable content is no easy task. The term "content" today refers to a variety of media, including podcasts, social media posts, videos, and blog articles. This is the part where we get to put your ideas to work.

You'll be ready to plan out your content calendar once you've narrowed down your topics and themes. Take a look at your calendar and decide what you'll be posting each week. That's the idea right here. I advise creating a content calendar that covers the next three months.

Avoid complicating things by scheduling an excessive number of postings each week. For instance, if you're just starting out, submit one new element once a week instead of attempting to publish two or three items each time. You can move straight to adding additional content after you develop a weekly publishing habit. You'll have mastered consistency by this point.

3. Keep to your schedule.
4. Repeat

Congratulations for studying till the end ... You , yes You, can make a hell of money just by following your dreams and passions. The key is to try as much as possible to surround yourself with the right set of people (Potential clients inclusive), build ,nurture your relationship with them and capitalize on that trust you have built by monetizing.
Have this at the back of your mind.... Anything sells, but only when you follow the right route. Go for knowledge.

See you at the top.
#Anticipate.

www.ingramcontent.com/pod-product-compliance
Lightning Source LLC
Chambersburg PA
CBHW070322220526
45465CB00013B/2166